Blogging through India

by

Robert A. Compton

Barbara –
Best wishes for a happy
2007 !

AuthorHouse™
1663 Liberty Drive, Suite 200
Bloomington, IN 47403
www.authorhouse.com
Phone: 1-800-839-8640

AuthorHouse™ UK Ltd.
500 Avebury Boulevard
Central Milton Keynes, MK9 2BE
www.authorhouse.co.uk
Phone: 08001974150

First published by AuthorHouse 12/4/2006

ISBN: 978-1-4259-7808-2 (sc)

Library of Congress Control Number: 2006909962

Printed in the United States of America
Bloomington, Indiana

This book is printed on acid-free paper.

Bloomington, IN Milton Keynes, UK

authorHOUSE®

I get asked that question a lot. The answer is simple: There is an **economic tectonic shift taking place** and I want to see it up close for myself.

The moment that defined this shift for me occurred about two years ago. The state of Indiana, where I'd lived and worked for many years, awarded a multi-million software development contract to an Indian company called Tata Consulting.

The Author

This would not have seemed out of the ordinary, except for the fact that Indiana's economy was struggling and the government went all the way to India to spend Indiana taxpayer money. This in a state that graduates more Computer Science majors per capita than any other.

How could the bid from Tata be so compelling that the governor risked the public's wrath, which rained down on him? And the contract was subsequently rescinded.

I started to research that question and I learned that just because I do not know something big is happening, doesn't mean it's not—or something like that.

What I discovered for myself over the ensuing twenty-four months and what Thomas Friedman articulated in his book, *The World Is Flat*, earlier this year is that in the past ten years India and China in particular and Eastern Europe, South America, Southeast Asia, etc. in general had opened their economies to foreign investment and unleashed a highly motivated, well-educated, and very large "middle class" to compete beyond low-wage manufacturing jobs. In the span of ten years, three billion new capitalists joined the world economy.

The numbers are by now well known, but they were news to me a year ago: **China graduating 500,000 engineers annually, India graduating 250,000 engineers; the U.S. graduating about 70,000**, a significant number of whom are studying abroad from China, India, Singapore, Taiwan, etc.

In fact, in engineering, science, medicine and even the law India graduates four to five times as many students as the U.S. China alone graduates 1,000,000 more college student per year than the U.S.

Think about those numbers and multiply them by 5, 10 or 15 years and one can get a bit concerned about how competitive the job market is going to be in 2020.

But wait. The news gets worse. Not only are India and China turning out five times as many engineering graduates; **the starting salary for Indian engineers is about 20 percent of the starting salary for a freshly minted U.S. engineer.** With China, the salaries are about 10 percent.

So are the Indian engineers only 20 percent as smart at calculus? Or do they only work one fifth as hard as a U.S. engineer? That has not been my observation from a distance. It appears that Indian and Chinese engineers are every bit as smart as their American counterparts and actually seem to have a stronger work ethic.

Why visit India and not China? While I believe China will dominate the global economy after 2030— and China is maybe next year's trip— it seems to me that India will be dominant until then.

India has several natural advantages that China lacks for now. For starters, India is the largest English-speaking democracy in the world, with 1.1 billion people. Due to British rule they share the same legal underpinnings as the U.S.—although they haven't discovered the job-creation and wealth-transfer possibilities of the U.S. bar.

India's middle class, which numbers about 200 million, enjoys not only a national primary and secondary curriculum of very high standards (compared to the U.S.); the parents are deeply involved in the child's education and **there is a very strong culture to get ahead**—get a college degree.

In India, students and parents are held accountable for academic performance. Low achievement reflects negatively on the parents—not on the teachers, or the government, or society. Low achievement also means a child will not be promoted to the next grade. **No Failing Child Gets Ahead is India's emphasis, rather than No Child Left Behind.**

On Friday nights, when U.S. high school students are at football games with friends, Indian students are at home studying, because Saturday is a school day. When U.S. students head home at 3:00 p.m., Indian students still have two more hours of school. When U.S. students are in their first two months of summer break, Indian students are still at school.

When U.S. students wonder where "American" jobs went, Indian students will be gainfully employed.

So this is what I've read and heard about India. On Wednesday I start the journey to find out for myself: **What is going on in India?**

Here's the plan:

Memphis to Detroit - 2 hrs, 90 minute layover, Detroit to Amsterdam - 8hrs, 2 hour layover, Amsterdam to Delhi - 8 hrs, clear customs 1 hr, Delhi airport to Oberoi hotel - 1 hr (I hope)

Door-to-door - 24 hours

Spend a couple days in **Delhi**. Oberoi Delhi Hotel

Fly to **Bangalore**.
Couple days in Bangalore with our friends at HealthAsyst. Windsor Manor

Fly to **Mumbai**
Day and a half in Mumbai. Taj Mahal Palace Hotel

Drive to **Jaipur**.
Day and a half in Jaipur. Raj Palace Hotel

Drive to **Bharatpur**, spend night. The Bagh Resort

Drive to **Agra** - sunset at Taj Mahal Oberoi Amavilas Hotel
Day in Agra

Drive to **Delhi** for two more days. Oberoi Delhi Hotel
Fly Delhi to Amsterdam, Amsterdam to Memphis.

India is a land of 1.1 billion people, 700 million of whom are Hindu, 200 million Muslim, with the remaining 200 million a mixture of Buddhist, Sikh, Jain, Christian, and Jewish.

Going with the majority, I ask Lord Ganesha for a safe and educational journey with minimal obstacles to overcome.

Ganesha, or Ganapati, is an extremely popular God in India. He is the Lord of and destroyer of obstacles. People mostly worship him asking for **siddhi** (success in undertakings) and **buddhi** (intelligence). He is worshiped before any venture is started. He is also the god of education, knowledge and wisdom, literature, and the fine arts.

9:30 a.m., Amsterdam: I'm on a two-hour layover at the airport here, so a quick post.

I had a very interesting conversation on the flight over **with a top executive from GM**. This is a pretty depressing time for him: thirty-seven years with the company; tapped for this senior position a couple years ago, and then all hell is breaking loose.

While we waited to take off he got several calls, the first one was telling him GM had just announced a restatement of 2001 earnings and the *Wall Street Journal* was not taking it well. Next was a new issue with the SEC (which he obviously did not disclose) and finally an update on Delphi—that the UAW was going to dig in its heels and ride Delphi all the way to liquidation rather than accept globally competitive wages. In the UAW's view, no jobs are better than jobs at nine dollars an hour. He said it was a "pride thing."

So after he had a couple stiff drinks, we talked about how the auto industry got here. To summarize a long and very interesting discussion, the union-management "relationship," which may have worked when there was little global competition, has become a chokehold on the industry. **GM is at a permanent cost disadvantage** due to union pay scales, inflexible work rules, "payoffs, not layoffs," U.S. health care costs, and an extraordinarily large pension obligation.

It may have been the Scotch talking, but he is not optimistic that GM will avoid bankruptcy. The UAW will certainly strike Delphi as Miller closes U.S. plants, and in his view the UAW can "bring GM to its knees within weeks."

"So how is this all going to turn out?" I asked.

"It looks like federal, state, and local governments are going to have share the burden of saving the U.S. auto industry."

I asked, If the clock could be turned back thirty years, what GM could have done differently? Answer: Outsource more aggressively, off-shore sooner (GM has almost no meaningful operation in India or China.), don't build so many plants in the U.S., and management should have taken a tougher, more realistic line on co-pays and defined retirement benefits.

To top off his depression, Detroit appears to have re-elected the mayor that has plunged the city into a 300-million-dollar deficit. Two thousand people per week are moving out of the Detroit city limits, and likely the city will have to file for the municipal equivalent of bankruptcy.

On the bright side, his kids are grown and living happily outside of Michigan and thankfully they are not in the auto industry. And his house is paid off.

4:00 am, New Delhi: From Amsterdam to Delhi I had an entirely different experience. Sitting next to me was **an upper middle manager from Microsoft.** Summarizing his most interesting points:

1- He was born in India, but as his father worked for the UN, he lived all over the world: the U.S., Europe, South America. And he attended some of the top private schools for diplomats. They moved back to India for his junior and senior year of high school.

2- I asked how he did on his Central Board of Secondary Education exams to get into eleventh grade. He sheepishly admitted that his father had to use diplomat influence to have him accepted back into an Indian high school and that he didn't fair all that well. He went on to a business college in Mumbai.

3- He lives in Seattle now and is happily married to an American woman. He has no intention of ever returning to India to live, but enjoys going back to visit and to support Microsoft's growing presence.

4- He admitted that Microsoft was significantly behind other large corporations in outsourcing to India, but things are accelerating. They have built a huge software R&D center here that is doing extraordinary work and they have another couple thousand developers and a small but growing pool of back-office workers in several cities.

5- He was very enthusiastic about Bill Gates's recent announcement about Web 2.0 services and was a real fan of Ray Ozzie. Microsoft has been late to the services game, but "when you generate one billion dollars in cash per month, you can devote a lot of resources to catching up fast—internal growth or acquisition."

He was clearly a very smart, enthusiastic, optimistic person. On the topic of whether America can stay competitive in engineering and manufacturing with India and China, he was less sanguine. His point was "the sheer volume of engineers and scientists that these two countries produce just dwarfs America. At some point in time the numbers become overwhelming and insurmountable."

7:00 a.m. Delhi: Well, after a refreshing three hours of sleep, I started my morning tour of Delhi with a delightful guide named Mahli. She is a PhD in Indian history. She's been great. I ask an endless stream of questions and she has very interesting answers with lots of historical context.

We took a driving and walking tour around the government buildings. The British influence is apparent in both the architecture and the street layout. The boulevards are very wide and straight, with beautiful trees on either side.

Traffic was not very bad; a lot less than I had imagined. Lots of very small cars (mostly Japanese, Korean), lots of motorcycles, bicycles everywhere, and hundreds of these three-wheeled motorized taxis.

They do drive on the left-hand side of the road. And on the right. And often down the middle. I've seen several public service signs proclaiming "Lane Driving Is Sane Driving." They are ignored.

Weather is great—blue sky, seventy degrees, slight breeze, and low humidity.

Mahli has sent me to take my nap. More later.

Typical Delhi street scene

10:00 p.m., Delhi: This afternoon had many interesting and inspiring aspects. First, we spent an hour or so at a Sikh temple. One removes one's shoes, washes one's feet, and quietly enters the temple. All are welcome and there are a wide variety of worshipers present.

Some say short prayers, give an offering of food or flowers, and then head back to work or other activities. Many sit around the open square room (there are no pews) and are in deep contemplation and prayer.

Three musicians play soothing music, although using instruments with which I'm unfamiliar. It was a very peaceful and relaxing sound.

Nearby is another large square room with an open kitchen where the faithful are busy preparing lunch for any who are hungry. All are welcome.

I did talk with three lepers—one young woman and two men. They are careful not to touch you and I gave each some money. Leprosy is a horribly disfiguring and ultimately fatal disease. The Sikh worshippers obviously know these three and give them food every day.

Next we visited the shrine on the site where Gandhi was assassinated. He was fatally shot in the backyard of a friend's house as he went to bless a gathering of people and lead them in prayer. The memorial is made of cast footprints that lead down a path and stop at a small shrine marking where he fell. Many Indians come to pay their respects to a man who is clearly a national and international hero of nonviolent change.

Finally we went a little way outside Delhi to an enormous complex of beautiful and impressive Hindu temples. Hundreds were there praying and I learned that most Hindus pray two to three times a day at a nearby temple or in a small shrine they create at home.

It is very easy to sense the deep spirituality of the Indian people. It is reflected in their shrines but also in their demeanor, which is calm and quiet. Everyone has a gracious way of greeting someone new, by bringing their hands together as if in prayer and giving a slight bow and a smile.

It has been a most fulfilling and educational day.

4:00 a.m. New Delhi: Still trying to get on the local time zone, but since I'm up early I forgot to mention a conversation I had with my guide about personal economics.

Both she and her husband work and they are "in middle class," in her words. They have one fifteen-year-old daughter. As a guide, her work is cyclical with the travel season and my sense is she doesn't work every day.

I don't know how much Mahli makes (I have some decorum), but she had said **the young people who work at U.S. call centers make very good money —"about $800 U.S. per month."**

My guess is, between her and her husband, they earn $30,000 per year, and the income tax rate is around 30 percent at that level, if I understood her correctly.

Now here's the good part: They had lived most of their lives in a small apartment but recently built and own a home outside the city. They have a live-in "servant" who cooks, cleans, and takes care of the house. Mahli has a driver who also does the daily shopping—for fresh vegetables and meats. The family's clothes are picked up regularly to be cleaned and ironed. And they have a man who takes care of the yard and other maintenance.

BTW, she and her husband never dated, as **hers was an arranged marriage**. ("Yes, of course" she said when I asked.) Her daughter does not date. "No, no, no. Of course not. Girls only go out with friends in large groups." Nor will she ever date, as Mahli and her husband will arrange a marriage for her someday.

We talked a bit about the ramifications of this. There are also almost no out-of-wedlock children. There is also very little divorce in India. That's not to say every relationship is happy; just that societal pressures are to stay together and raise your children. If there is a single parent it is because the other has died.

My guide in Delhi

9:30 a.m., Delhi: The front page news in *The Economic Times* this morning was "Business Plan Contest to Fetch Rs 16 Lakh in Prize Money" (Rs = rupees, Lakh = 100,000 Rupees; winners will split about $37,000 in prize money) The contest is sponsored by the Indian Institute of Management Ahmedabad, the top B-school in India and arguably among the top in the world.

Founded in 1961 with significant involvement from Harvard Business School, IIM-Ahmedabad has 250 students (culled from 150,000 applications annually). The HBS influence is seen in the 100 percent case-method pedagogy. Perhaps their most famous graduate known to U.S. business people is University of Michigan professor and management guru, **C.K. Prahalad.**

For the past six years, IIM-A has hosted a large and rather complex business competition. There are eight competitive judged events, including a Business Case competition, a stock market competition, and a team business plan competition, which appears to be the highlight. Students will test their ability to conceive and plan a new venture.

I noted with great disappointment that the cocktail reception will NOT be competitive. Sure, take away the one skill area where U.S. MBAs can dominate.

You can learn more about confluence on the Web site www.iima-confluence.com. I noted Purdue has been invited to compete. It will be interesting to watch how they rank.

What jumps out at me from this contest and the fact that it is front-page news in Delhi (IIM-A is on the west coast of India.) is that **Indians are intensely eager to hone their entrepreneurial and new venture-creation skills** and they love to compete against all comers. Hmm....

1:00 a.m., Delhi: I spent an unbelievable day in Old Delhi, which I thought could not be topped, but I'll have to write about that tomorrow.

This afternoon I was introduced to a terrific young investment banker with Jefferies International named Mickey Commar. Not only was he kind enough to invite me to his family's house for dinner; he invited me on the evening he was **meeting the parents of a young woman in the getting-acquainted stage of the arranged marriage process**. Mickey has not yet met the woman, although scouting reports from friends are promising and her parents could not be more delightful.

I felt extremely honored and privileged to be included in such a consequential dinner. I don't believe I have felt more welcome, at home and graciously included than I did tonight with these two families.

I have a flight to Bangalore in a few hours and need to get some sleep, so I'll write more tomorrow.

For now I'll say:

1) **Arranged marriages have more merit to them than meets the eye.** (I may be a convert, Elizabeth and Meredith.)

2) The family dynamics are changing in Indian culture as young adults earn more, have more career options, and leave India.

3) Home-cooked Indian food is truly fantastic.

4) The Sikh's are very warm, hospitable, entertaining, and fascinating people, and

5) Mickey's prospective father-in-law promised: If I can help close the deal, I have an invitation to my first Indian wedding.

9:00 p.m. Delhi - It takes a visit to Old Delhi to fully appreciate that **this is a city of 13 million diverse, busy people.** Whereas New Delhi feels like Washington, D.C.—large government buildings, wide boulevards, tree-lined parks, police patrols, and a general sense of order. Old Delhi is chaotic, dense, dramatic, compelling, and unlike any place in the Western world.

Hundreds of streets (as narrow as five feet across) are teaming with bicycles, motor-rickshaws, horse-drawn carts, cows, motor scooters, tricycle rickshaws, tiny cars, thousands and thousands of people on foot, and the occasional elephant.

The biggest SUV in Delhi

Ancient five-story buildings line the streets, packed with tiny five-by-eight shops that spill into the crowd. Thickets of power cables and telephone wires grow like vines overhead. Occasionally monkeys and squirrels scamper across the lines. Street dogs wander along looking for scraps. And a rat darts here and there.

Beautiful women float along draped in brilliant, flowing colors. Laughing children scamper underfoot and workmen balance bolts of bright cloth, sacks of grain, piles of vegetables, or bundles of wood on their heads.

Muslim women, hidden in elegant black cloth with only their eyes revealed, move as fluidly through the crowds as proud Sikh men with their vibrant, bright turbans.

A melody of Hindi voices selling products, negotiating prices, and ordering food fills the air that is also steeped with smells: spices, cooking oil, charcoal, smoke, steaming vegetables, incense, and curried chicken.

What I didn't see or hear were crying children, parents yelling, anger, tension, shoving, rudeness, or anything other than gracious, busy people—a whole LOT of people!

Old Delhi street scene

9:30 p.m. Delhi: **These guys wrote the book on salesmanship.** Every sales rep should apprentice in a Kashmiri rug merchant's shop.

Before leaving Delhi I thought I'd look at some silk carpets. Here's a greatly abridged transcript of **an entertaining and expensive three hours.**

Wani: Please sir, come in…sit. May I ask your name?

Me: My name is Bob. I just want to look around.

Wani: No, no, no…please sir, Mr. Bob, first you must sit, relax, have some wonderful Kashmiri tea—like nothing you have ever tasted. We must talk and get to know one another.

Me: Well, maybe one cup of tea…

Wani (wheeling out a full-sized carpet loom): All our carpets are handmade by families in Kashmir. Some carpets take seven, eight, ten years for a family to complete. Every design done by hand, then coded onto dozens of long strips of paper—each page showing what color for each knot. One carpet—4' x 6'—contains 1.3 million knots. [He goes on to give a thirty-minute demo showing exactly how a loom rug is woven and trimmed. I'm absolutely entranced.]

Wani: Now Mr. Bob, I present to you…the finest work of my home country of Kashmir… [Four sons appear, each pair holding a large rolled carpet. On Wani's sharp command, the carpets are simultaneously unfurled in a way that makes a fine "pop" as they hit the floor and unroll to within an inch of my feet. I'm awed.]

Wani: Mr. Bob, these are the finest carpets of Kashmir.

Me: How much do they cost?

Wani: Mr. Bob…what price is there for art? These carpets will last two hundred years. Tell me how many rooms in your house?

For the next hour I see over one hundred rugs, all dramatically unfurled by four now sweating sons. Each carpet is unique, beautiful and I still don't know the price. So I cut to the chase...

Me: I'd like two rugs—one very small, all silk and one 4' x 6' silk and Kashmir wool ("the finest wool in all the world").

After about twenty minutes, I finally hear the price.... (I'm shocked.)

Me: I think maybe only one rug....

Wani: Mr. Bob, I like you very much; we make a deal.

The price comes down just enough to re-hook me.

Wani: Now we have a deal. If you will just sign here...

My Trusted Guide: Don't sign that...I will talk to his boss. [She proceeds to have a thirty-minute negotiation in Hindi with the boss, a large, scary-looking man in a giant caftan.]

The price comes down 40 percent, so with a nod from My Trusted Guide, I sign the deal.

Wani: Now Mr. Bob...I want to show you the finest silk scarves in all the world made by hand by Kashmiri families...

Note to my wife: Expect a somewhat larger than intended UPS package next week. Please pay the MasterCard bill as soon as possible. **And remember, they will last two hundred years. :-)**

10:00 p.m., Bangalore: It was another extraordinary day—this time in Bangalore. There may be no such a thing as an ordinary day in India. There's way too much happening, too fast.

Bangalore is Silicon Valley to Delhi's Washington, D.C. Information technology businesses dominate the city and blanket the landscape: GE, IBM, Oracle, EMC, Accenture, HP, Intel, E&Y, Microsoft, KPMG, Philips, Siemens, PWC—just to name a few. And all with 10, 15, 20,000 employees and growing fast.

We spent the afternoon at HP. Across India they have 18,000 employees with 10,000 in Bangalore. **They plan to hire another 3,000 engineers in 2006.** Yes, they do basic call-center work, but that's just entry level for the new engineering graduates ($7,500 starting salary).

HP Global Delivery Applications Services does a WHOLE lot more. Level 1, 2 and 3 support—in 10 languages—24/7/365. Application development, remote diagnostics, a giant network operating center, systems deployment, and a bunch of sophisticated stuff I didn't understand.

HP runs forty-one overlapping shifts per day (waves of people coming and going around the clock). The campus has seven to eight enormous buildings—four completed in the past eighteen months. There is on-site food around the clock (including Dominos Pizza), a full gym, an enormous training facility, and dormitories (for people working on major projects to get some sleep). They even have their own buses to pick up and deliver employees from home every day.

Their campus is located in **Electronics City,** along with hundreds of other IT companies. Inside the city, things are modern and well built. Between Bangalore proper and EC, however, it is a complete mess. Traffic was like nothing I've ever seen. The roads are a disaster: rutted, potholes, no traffic signals, no shoulders, etc. Rush hour was like a crazy, congested road race across Baja. Even the cows looked nervous.

So with tens of thousands of engineers being hired every year (and growing), I wondered if the "well of talent" would soon run dry. It turns out, like good engineers, the industry has modeled that question and determined they have seven years of "supply" before reaching the current engineer supply limit.

BUT, pressed by the IT industry, **the Indian government is busy building new colleges** that will graduate engineers specializing in IT services. The industry is co-developing the curriculum so that graduates will be productive much faster. These colleges will begin delivering thousands of additional engineers well before 2012, keeping the well full and salaries down.

So it doesn't look very likely that the compensation of Indian IT workers will approach Western pay scales any time soon and make outsourcing less economic.

We do have nicer roads.

11:00 p.m., Bangalore: We had the great pleasure of visiting Allscripts' (www.allscripts.com) software development partners here in Bangalore: **HealthAsyst (http://www.healthasyst.com).**

What an impressive group of young, enthusiastic, smart engineers, MDs, MBAs, and CPAs. Spending a few hours with them was tremendously energizing.

The HealthAsyst Team

HealthAsyst was started by Umesh Bajaj, an engineer (of course), who spent twenty years working his way up the IT services management ladder at a variety of IT companies.

Umesh started his company (funded entirely from his own savings) in the mid-1990s, and he survived the IT downturn when a lot of Indian entrepreneurs raced back to the security of a salary at the large IT companies. He's a true entrepreneur.

Reflecting on what impressed me the most about this clearly impressive group, here's what I saw:

Umesh and me

1- Articulate: To a person, the HealthAsyst employees were crisp, clear, and compelling in their observations and suggestions.

2- Enthusiasm for hard work: When asked, What can we do better as partners? the most frequent responses were: Give us more challenges, stretch our capabilities, engage us more in the creative process.

3- Continuous education: Every Friday the entire HA team meets at 5:00 p.m. for an hour of technical presentations and fun group games that challenge their creativity. After each session they go back to work for another hour or two. After all, it's only a Friday night.

At a fabulous dinner Umesh hosted, Glen and I participated in the sort of activities the group does every Friday evening. The forty-plus of us were randomly divided into teams for two "acting" challenges. Each team was a given a phrase—in our case, "electronic tag"—around which **we had to create a skit** that illustrated the device, explained how it might be applied in a novel way to healthcare, and act out the scene so as to sell the audience on the device's merits and be amusing and entertaining—with every team member playing a role.

We had five minutes to brainstorm ideas, assign roles, and develop a story line that could be performed in two minutes.

What was amazing was **the engagement, creativity, and absence of inhibition**. Probably I should not have been surprised, but I was struck by the joy, humor, and enthusiasm from this very highly educated, technical group.

In our scene, I played the part of the ailing, elderly patient (type-casting) who nearly dies because the hospital has not invested in the lifesaving information capabilities of an electronic tag. Fortunately, my team members were able to close the sale in time to save my life.

Scene from a sales skit

It was a great icebreaker and a great way to get everyone thinking in creative ways about healthcare technologies. Here is a picture of the HealthAsyst team and a few pictures from the sales melodramas the five teams delivered.

Over dinner I had the chance to talk with many of the HealthAsyst employees. I was interested and **delighted to see so many women engineers**. Several of them, who were out of college less than two years, related when they decided to go into engineering. "Since I was twelve or thirteen, I wanted to be an engineer. Almost all of the girls at school wanted to be engineers or doctors. It is the best profession in India."

I decided to verify that early interest in engineering for myself, so Umesh arranged for us to visit a K-12 private school in Bangalore, where his son had attended. It is the Indian equivalent of the school my daughters attend, St. George's School in Germantown, Tennessee.

Stayed tuned for what I learned.

11:00 p.m., Bangalore: When we visited the national public school of Bangalore, I felt like the college football scout who'd snuck in to watch a rival team's practice, ready to record their training secrets.

Like in the U.K., "public" school actually means private school, and in India about 30 percent of the families pay directly for their education. Another 50 percent of students attend government-run schools and roughly 20 percent of the kids have no formal schooling. Education is not compulsory yet in India, so roughly 100 million kids aren't even in the race—that's twice the U.S. student population still to join the competition.

Here's my scouting report: The other team puts in 40 percent MORE practice time per year than our team—more hours per day, more days per week, more months per year. Their "workouts" are more rigorous in math, science, and language. They "scrimmage" at every opportunity and they set inviolable standards for staying on the team.

Rather than No Child Left Behind, in India it's **No Child Gets Ahead Without Hard Work and Demonstrated Accomplishment**. (I know it sounds crazy, but they actually hold students back and no lawsuits are filed.)

Student failure is seen first as the failure of the student (huh?), then as a failure of the parents (what?!). It is not seen as a failure of the teacher or school, or in any way George Bush's fault (sorry Glen).

Now, I'm happy to report not all the news is grim. Our buildings are much bigger and nicer; we have the best athletic facilities; our refreshment stands are better stocked and our cheerleaders have cuter outfits.

Next post: details of our visit.

NPS's Multi-Sport Athletic Complex

11:30 p.m., Bangalore: Our friend Umesh was kind enough to arrange a meeting for us with Ms. Shantha Chandran, Associate Principal at National Public Schools, Bangalore.

NPS is the Bangalore equivalent of St. George's Schools in Memphis, where my two daughters attend. NPS is **a for-profit, family-owned business**. Shantha has been at NPS for twenty-seven years and was very happy to describe their program.

Ms. Shantha

Students start school at age two and a half with the Montessori program that runs through age six. In grades one through five, the students attend school five days per week, ten months out of the year.

In sixth grade, things get a little tougher. School starts before 8:00 a.m. and ends about 3:30 p.m., **six days per week, ten and a half months out of the year**.

The curriculum consists of math, biology, chemistry, physics, history, English, Hindi, and the local language.

At this age, kids are already starting to prepare for their **CBSE exams** in tenth grade—an exam that must be passed in all **eight subjects tested three hours each** or the student does not go to eleventh grade.

When asked the aspect of the school of which she was most proud, Shantha immediately took us to the "cyber lab": rooms filled with computers, a student working diligently at each terminal.

Computer room – 8th grade

I asked if we might see the athletic facilities and Shantha showed us the dirt playground behind the school.

"Ah-ha," I said, "so the kids get no physical education; they're just a bunch of bookworms."

Shantha: Oh, that's not accurate, Mr. Bob. We have physical education classes including cricket, basketball, karate, track, and volleyball. We just do not make it our highest priority. Academic study is our primary mission."

I retort, "I see…so it's all books and a little cricket. No truly creative activities, I'll bet."

Shantha: Oh, that's not true, Mr. Bob. The students take many art, music, and creative writing classes throughout their fourteen years here. The creative activities are emphasized in the early years and in ninth, tenth, eleventh, and twelfth grades math, physics, chemistry, and biology are emphasized.

"But all this study makes pretty dull and one-dimensional students, don't you think?" says I.

Shantha: Ah, Mr. Bob, but I have not mentioned our extra-curricular activities of which each child must be involved—one each semester. Groups like the Shakespeare club, the debate team, band, choir, fine arts, tae kwon do, computer club, art workshops, etc.

"Do the students have any chance to do public speaking. You know that's a strength of the U.S. system," I mentioned, now a bit tentative.

Shantha: Oh yes, Mr. Bob, *everyone* is required to make speeches in school up to sixth grade. After that the students are encouraged to give talks and presentations, but it is not required. The students that have that gift or a strong desire have plenty of speaking opportunities.

She continued, "Students are also encouraged to participate in our inter-school competitions in elocution, declamation, debate, science quiz, logic quiz, creative writing in Hindi and English, Western vocal, classical dance, painting, and Indian vocal."

Concluding, she stated, "Of course, everyone competes to participate in the National and International Olympiads in math, physics, chemistry, biology, and cyber . We have won several trophies, if you would like to see them…."

"So when do kids hang out at the mall?" I asked.

Shantha: I do not understand your question, Mr. Bob.

"You don't have a football team, do you?"

Shantha: No, Mr. Bob. You have us there. We have no football team.

Morning inspection

Library time

Senior classroom

First grade classroom

Changing classes

I asked Shantha about college and careers her students intended to pursue.

"By the time they are in high school, eighty percent of my students want to be engineers. It has been that way ever since I started teaching. But don't take my word for it. Go ask our students."

We did just that. Glen and I went to several classrooms of our choosing—a first grade, an eighth grade—and we stopped several seniors at random. Here's what we found in this non-scientific sample (I have this on videotape.):

6 - Engineers
3 - Military (This is a highly prestigious and competitive career in India.)
2 - Doctors
2 - Teachers
2 - Artists
1 - Entrepreneur
1 - Interior Designer
1 - Accountant
1 - Astronomer
1- Astronaut (India has a growing space program.)

Based on our conversations with the older students, it is easy to see that by grade nine, engineering and medicine will be the dominant interests.

I questioned Shantha about what had changed most over the past twenty-seven years. Her response was that **the level of competition has risen dramatically** because of an enormous increase in the number of families that can now afford primary education.

"There are only so many seats at the top engineering schools, so everyone is pushing harder, earlier to get in to the Indian Institute of Technology, tutoring, and extra math classes start as early as fifth grade.

"I worry that parents put too much pressure on their children to excel in academics. They are not as concerned about interpersonal behavior and social graces as parents were twenty years ago. "

Bob: And if they don't get in to IIT, what happens?

Shantha: They all have their **safety schools**, of course. In 2004, my students who fell short of IIT standards went on to attend Carnegie Mellon, Princeton, University of Pennsylvania, UCLA, University of Minnesota, and Purdue University in Indiana.

Bob: Oh...okay, can we see the cafeteria now?

11:45 p.m., Bangalore: Glen and I consider ourselves pretty capable salesmen, but we were repeatedly humbled in the presence of sales greatness in India.

Regardless of city, the Indian sales person has an array of tried-and-true techniques for what I call the **Indian structured sales call**.

1- People Do Business with People They Like - Shopping is a process, not an event, in India. Every shop we entered insisted we sit, have tea or coffee and some food, and visit a bit before the clerks started selling. After a while I got quite used to this and enjoyed these conversations of getting to know the owner.

2- Entry Level Price Point - Every Indian vendor, regardless of product, starts their pitch with an initially good-looking *product one* that is priced at a point that sounds very appealing.

3- The Upsell - As one starts to make the buy decision, the "better quality" product, *product two*, is presented. Now, while product one looked perfectly fine by itself, in comparison, product two puts it to shame.

4- The Best Quality - Having settled on product two, the final, top-of-the-line, best quality *product three* appears—and you have no choice but to buy it.

5- The "Just for Looking Only" Gambit - This is the hail mary of Indian sales: the vastly superior *product four* at ten times the price of product three. It is generally introduced as "now this is art, not merchandise." I never succumbed to this ploy, but my guess is, one out ten times, someone buys "art."

6 - The Cross Sell - No Indian vendor misses a chance to follow the initial purchase with a companion product—earrings to go with the necklace, fine Kashmiri scarves to go with the sari, a small carpet for your closet to go with the large bedroom carpet. I can attest to the sales uplift this strategy produces.

7 - The Kingfisher Variation - When the customer declines tea, the store offers a glass of the rich, tasty Indian Kingfisher beer. This conveys great hospitality and loosens the customer's purchase inhibitions. I saw this used only once, but to great affect. (Refer to my post *Damn, They Sell Carpets in Jaipur Too.*)

8 – "Let Me Introduce My Father" - Now they wheel out the **BIG GUN** of Indian selling: DAD! While you thought you were dealing with the forty-ish owner, the master is about to go to work. Don't worry, it's over very quickly....

9 - The Marble Sales Inversion - This is important. The only exception to the Indian structured sales call is in hand-cut inlaid marble. Here they start with the largest and most expensive pieces. The reason is, if they showed you the cheap stuff first, which is exquisite, you'd spend a tenth of what you might spend. Ask to see all three showrooms **BEFORE** you make the first marble purchase. I know what I'm talking about. I have a hand-cut, inlaid marble table arriving any day now.

There are twelve more steps to the Indian structured sales call, which are contained in my new book, *My Father Would Like You to Have This Beer.*

1:00 a.m., Bangalore: One spends a lot of time sitting in traffic in India, so a wide variety of entertainment and excitement comes right up to your car window.

So far, the cobra has been the most exciting. Glen snapped this shot, while I fumbled for my camera.

1:30 a.m., Bangalore: Umesh was kind enough to arrange for us to visit with the director of the Indian Institute of Management in Bangalore.

IIM was the first disappointment on the trip for me. I was absolutely certain their MBA program would have a heavy emphasis on entrepreneurship, thinking that the key to India's long-term growth must be new venture creation.

I was wrong. **The school has only two courses in entrepreneurship,** and although they have ten labs to incubate new technology start-ups, only four are in use. While the IIM in Ahmedabad has a very strong entrepreneurship curriculum, India's "Silicon Valley" does not.

The director offered why he thought there was so little interest among students in starting a new business or at least joining one upon graduation:

1- **Sixty percent of IIM students have engineering undergraduate degrees** and have survived the intensely competitive Indian education system. They are highly desirable recruits for large multi-national corporations, investment banks, and global consulting firms.

2- These employers offer Western-level compensation in overseas assignments. Each graduate has a minimum of three job offers, with the top offer in 2004 being $160,000 (for a UK post).

3- Students contrast these starting salaries with the pay that smaller enterprises can afford and choose to go to large enterprises.

4- IIM-Bangalore only graduates 125 MBAs annually, so there is limited "supply" to meet enormous demand.

5- The director also felt many of his graduates would ultimately start their own ventures but are practical enough to realize they need workplace experience, a network of contacts, and specific industry knowledge first.

6- Start-up capital is still relatively scarce in India, so funding a new technology company is tough (although several funds have started in B'glore and a dozen California VC's have established at least a presence).

So while I've found many Indians want to own their own business, the IIM will likely be turning out MBA's for the Global Fortune 1000 for many years to come.

2:00 a.m., Bangalore: Seeing all of the major U.S. technology companies hiring hundreds of thousands of Indians to produce products for sale back to the U.S., I began to worry a bit about what products U.S. workers might be producing that are of significant value to Indians.

I saw tons of Korean, Chinese, Japanese, and Taiwanese products everywhere. In twelve days I saw only one U.S. automobile. GM does own Opel, correct? What in the world are we going to sell Indians to pay for all that we buy from them?

I needn't have been concerned. Two of our major high-value corporations are already making rapid in-roads here in India, helping to ensure that while Americans are buying semi-conductor chips, sophisticated IT hardware, and advanced software from India, U.S. trade will be balanced by what Indians buy from us.

May I super-size those curry fries for you, kind sir?

At the mall in Bangalore

2:30 a.m., Bangalore: Through an introduction by one of Allscripts' very good U.S. customers, Glen and I were able to make a sales call while in Bangalore in Manipal Hospital, part of a large, first class, privately-owned healthcare system.

India has a **two-tiered healthcare system**: one government-run and one private-pay. As we saw at Manipal, the private-pay healthcare system is as good as anything in the U.S. and serves roughly 200 million people.

My impression of India's healthcare philosophy, based on very few data points, is that Indians believe the government should provide free, basic healthcare to the public, but not unlimited access to all therapies at any cost.

Medical Records Are Paper-Based
Glen Sees Sales Opportunity

Apparently the government recognizes that infinite healthcare coverage for 1.1 billion people is simply not affordable. Better to have quality basic care for everyone and allow those who can personally afford more to buy it from for-profit providers.

Manipal Hospital, Bangalore

After touring the Manipal facility—which is very impressive—we sat down with the CFO to start our sales pitch. Despite the fact that I offered no tea, Kingfisher beer, or tasty snacks, I did have a secret selling weapon: Glen Tullman.

Without a demo, without marketing materials, and really with no idea of how Manipal worked—but powered by *Glenergy salesmanship*—we managed to get a handshake deal with the CFO in less than one hour. He would not buy the Australian software he was about to purchase without thoroughly evaluating Allscripts' offering.

Manipal Hospital lobby

The Manipal experience taught me several things:

1- **India's middle class is as big as the U.S. middle class** and it is expanding at twice the pace. That means there are lots of business opportunities.

2- Except for McDonald's, KFC, Pepsi, Coke, Sheraton, and Hilton, most **American companies are missing in action** in this large and growing market.

3- **Someone is serving these customers**: the Australians, Japanese, Koreans, Singaporeans, and Chinese—just not the U.S. or Europe that I could tell.

4- **India is not wealthy (yet),** so selling products to them today requires innovative thinking about how to deliver quality at a price they can afford and when you can make a profit.

5- **Someday India will be wealthy**. It had an 8 percent GNP growth in '05; GNP growth projected at 10 percent for '06 and '07, compounding at 10 percent results in doubling the economy every seven years. Think back to the U.S. in the 1950's to get the idea.

6- Do you want to wake up in seven years, when India's economy has doubled and they can "afford" your U.S. prices, only to discover that the healthcare **software market is led by Australian and Japanese** companies, the **health insurance market is dominated by Chinese** companies, the **auto industry is led by Korea**, every corner coffee shop is a *KashmiriBucks*, etc.?

U.S. companies need **to think a bit long-term and build business foundations and relationships in India today**. There is no question in my mind that the return on this early investment will be substantial.

I've received several emails from readers (who lacked the courage to comment publicly), asking my views on a couple questions:

1- Will the outsourcing of knowledge work to India continue?

2- How do I know if my job is at risk?

3- What can I do to protect my job?

To answer the first question, I believe we have seen only the tip of the iceberg on Indian (and Chinese) outsourcing. The companies that have moved 10-20,000 jobs each to India that I mentioned in a previous post are really just the pioneers and early innovators.

They have worked out the logistics and communication issues, allowing the next wave of outsourcing by the more cautious corporations.

You'll also start to see Indian companies marketing more aggressively to small and mid-sized U.S. companies for outsourcing work.

Is Your Job At Risk?

I've created a simple **OUTSOURCING TEST** to assess your own vulnerability. Answer True or False to these 10 questions:

1. I spend at least five days per month in face-to-face interaction with our customers.
2. These face-to-face meetings cannot be done over the phone - value is added by my physical presence.
3. I am a nurse.
4. I am the first in the office to adopt new technologies or new processes to do my job more efficiently.
5. More than 25 percent of **HOW** I do my job is different this year than it was last year.
6. I am a janitor.
7. More than 33 percent of **WHAT** I do at work is different this year than last year.
8. I am intimately involved in the conception and creation of new products at work.
9. I am an avid reader of publications that keep me on the cutting edge of my profession.

10. I spend at least one day per month on education or experiences that will increase my capability to add unique value to my job.

If you answered True to more than 5 of the above questions, I would say you are safe for the next 5+ years.

Between 2-5 True, I'd have some anxiety; 1 or 2 True and you either are a nurse or janitor or you're in trouble.

If you answered zero True, you might consider how enthusiastically you can say **"Welcome to Wal-Mart."**

Next time: What can I do to protect My "American" job?

2:30 a.m., Bangalore: Everything I knew about the Hindu faith prior to this trip I learned from the Beatles and the Hare Krishna hippies at U.S. airports in the late '60s and early '70s.

Surprisingly, this was a rather incomplete picture of this fascinating religion.

Without detailing the specifics of Hindu, Sikh, or Jain faiths, let me simply share my impressions of having been to temple several times while in India.

1- **Always Open** - Temples seem to operate nearly 24/7, rather than just Sundays at 11:00 a.m. I joined 2,000 worshipers one evening at the Hare Krishna temple in Bangalore, hundreds of worshipers at a Sikh temple one afternoon in Delhi, and dozens of worshipers at the Jain temple one Thursday morning.

2- **Always Welcome** - I have rarely felt as welcome in a religious facility as I did in these temples.

3- **Non-Judgmental** - The Hindu, Sikh, and Jain faiths must be the least judgmental religions on earth. They seem to accommodate a wide range of personal views around a core set of beliefs and values. They also are quite accepting (much more than just tolerant) of other religions and beliefs.

4- **Temple As Total Experience** - The Hare Krishna temple reminded me in many ways of the huge churches in Memphis, with restaurants, gift shops, logo-clad T-shirts, and coffee shops all contained in the facility.

5- **Care For the Poor** - Let's face it: With 800 million people below the poverty line, India has serious challenges. I was quite impressed with the efforts made by the Hare Krishna temples to feed and educate the poor. - Akshaya Patra (http://www.akshayapatra.org).

I made a donation to their large Bangalore kitchen that feeds 120,000 local poor children each day. The meals are provided at the government schools as a way to draw the children to education.

I was particularly impressed with Akshaya Patra's commitment to transparency and accountability to donors. They document and publish their results (http://www.akshayapatra.org/documented_impact.html), which are verified by KPMG. Charities in the U.S. could take a lesson from them.

11:00 p.m., Elephanta Island, Mumbai: My apologies to my Indian friends. I should have removed my shoes.

I'm still learning, slowly. (I am American after all.)

11:30 p.m., Mumbai: 24 hours, 14 million people. Start shooting.

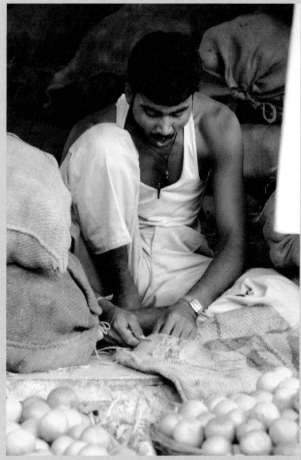

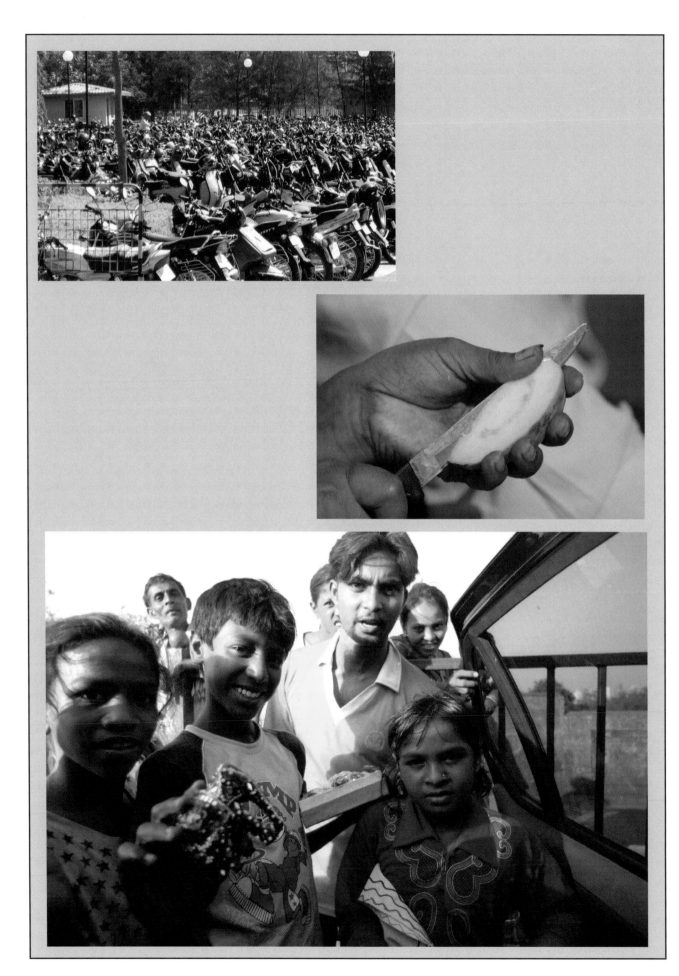

11:00 p.m., Mumbai: When we were in Mumbai, Glen and I had the good fortune to meet **an extraordinary entrepreneur named Ravi.**

Ravi moved to Mumbai eight years ago from a rural area, initially to start a retail sales business. In the subsequent years he also established a small manufacturing operation and a travel services business.

Ravi speaks nine languages at least conversationally: his native tongue, English, Hindi, French, Spanish, Italian, Portuguese, German, and Russian. Remarkably, he is entirely self-taught, although he has recently started taking night classes to broaden his education.

Ravi has a very warm, engaging personality and you instantly like him. With a quick sense of humor, he laughs easily and is a very talented raconteur.

Ravi

But I guess the thing that impressed us most about Ravi was this: **He is only twelve years old**.

That's right. He is just twelve years old. His grandmother brought him to Mumbai when he was four years old, apparently to help the rest of the family survive because economic conditions were so poor in his hometown.

With his then thirty-four-year-old grandmother, Ravi began selling little trinkets on the streets around the Hanging Gardens, a relatively clean and nice area on a hill overlooking Mumbai. Based on others we saw around that area, begging was likely their earliest means of survival.

Over the subsequent eight years, Ravi's natural-born talents emerged. He learned how to approach strangers and pitch them his product. Closing a sale, he then followed his customers around with their tour guides, learning not only their language but also the stories the guides told about the Hanging Gardens or the Tower of Silence or other sights.

As he made a little money, Ravi was able to buy raw materials for his grandmother to make fans of peacock feathers at night, which he could sell the next day, adding more profit to his sales.

Ravi is nothing if not fearless, and it was an easy step for him to suggest to trinket customers that they let him lead them through the gardens. He has a direct manner and a warm smile that are impossible to resist. Within a few years, Ravi could give a respectable tour of the gardens in a variety of languages.

He was very open to discussing his life and introducing us to his grandmother. He and his grandmother live in a tiny shack in the Mumbai slums, paying 3,000 rupees per month rent (about sixty dollars). Ravi does the grocery shopping and prepares the meals for the two of them.

Three nights a week, he goes to a teacher along with several other children to learn reading, writing, and arithmetic. They have no books and the "blackboard" is the dirt on the floor. He pays for these classes, but I can't recall the cost.

He does own two books *that he purchased*, and he is very proud of them. They weren't titles we recognized, but they were a very big deal to him.

He is excellent at mental math—quickly adding up prices for a variety of product combinations he was pitching us; then converting rupees to dollars at forty-five rupees per dollar. (Glen and I checked his math, but we were a lot slower.) My guess is he can do a similar conversion for euros or pounds sterling.

I asked Ravi what he wanted to be when he grew up: "I would liked to be a certified tour guide." The government regulates the number of tour guides and it is a respectable, well-paying career.

Glen asked him what he would do if he had a LOT of money, and without hesitation, here was his reply:

Ravi: First, I would give money to the people I know around here that need it more than I do. Then I would give some of it to Indians I don't know but who are poor. And the rest I would keep for myself.

Glen: What would you do with your money?

Ravi: I would buy a business.

Glen: Would you buy a small retail business?

Ravi: Oh no, I would buy a very big business in the oil industry. The oil business is very important and I would buy a big oil company.

After and hour or so, we had to say goodbye to Ravi and his grandmother. Needless to say, we bought a lot of his peacock fans and we paid him very well for giving us perhaps the most inspiring tour either Glen or I had ever experienced.

If you are in Mumbai, go to the Hanging Gardens and look for this extraordinary boy. It will be the most educational, inspiring, and fun hour you'll spend in Mumbai. And ask him to tell the story of the Tower of Silence. You'll be fascinated.

Ravi and his grandmother

"If you want interesting pictures, stand in front of interesting subjects."

- Joe McNally, National Geographic Photographer

I continue to be entirely captivated by the beauty, character, and purity of the Indian people. Glen suggested I just post the photos without comment.

I'll let the expressions speak for themselves.

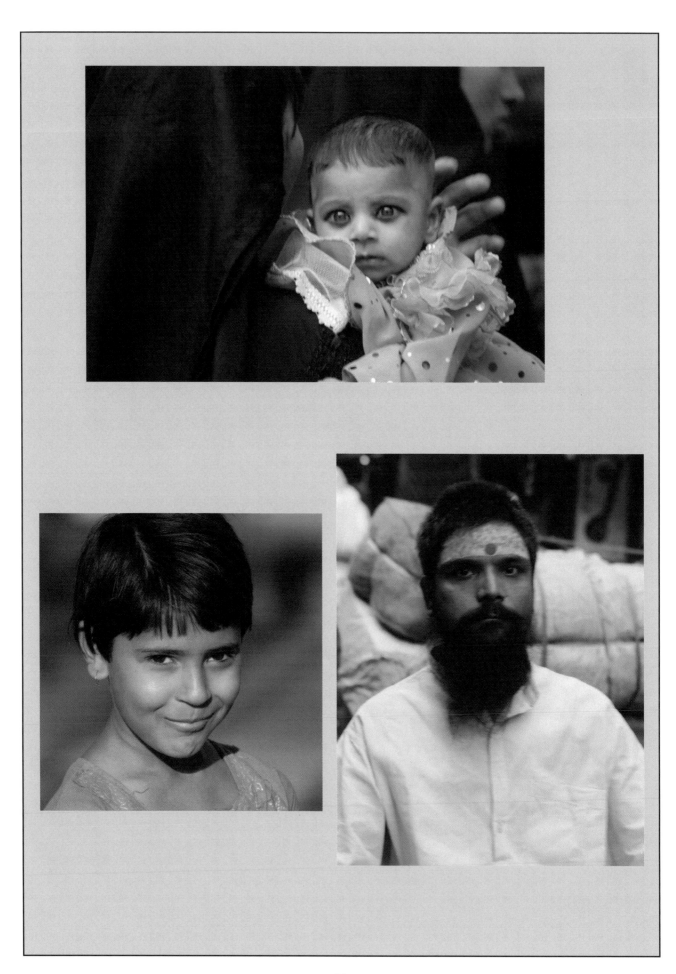

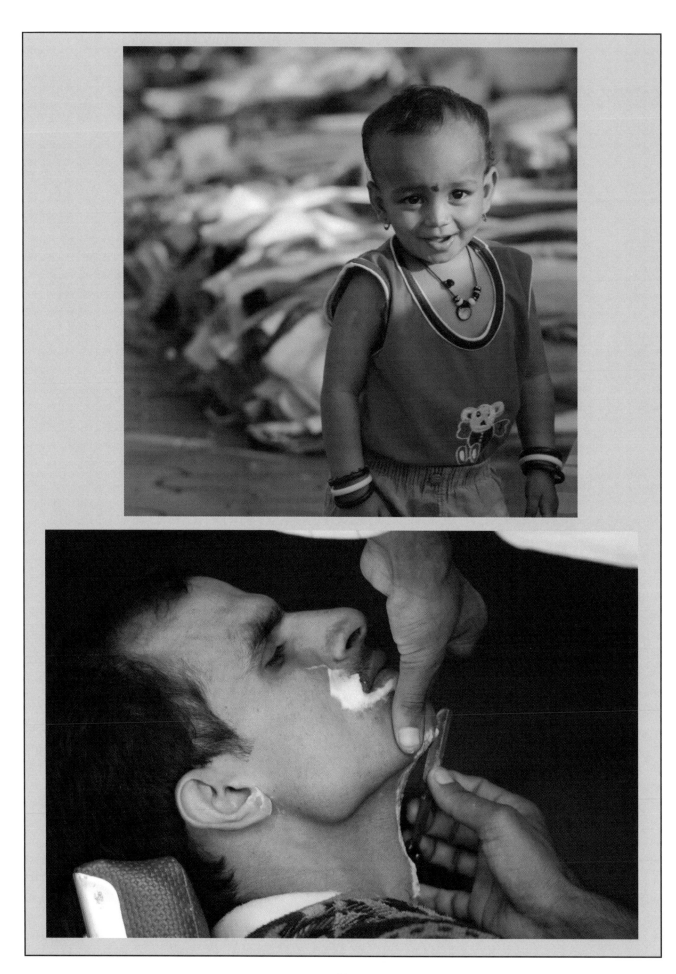

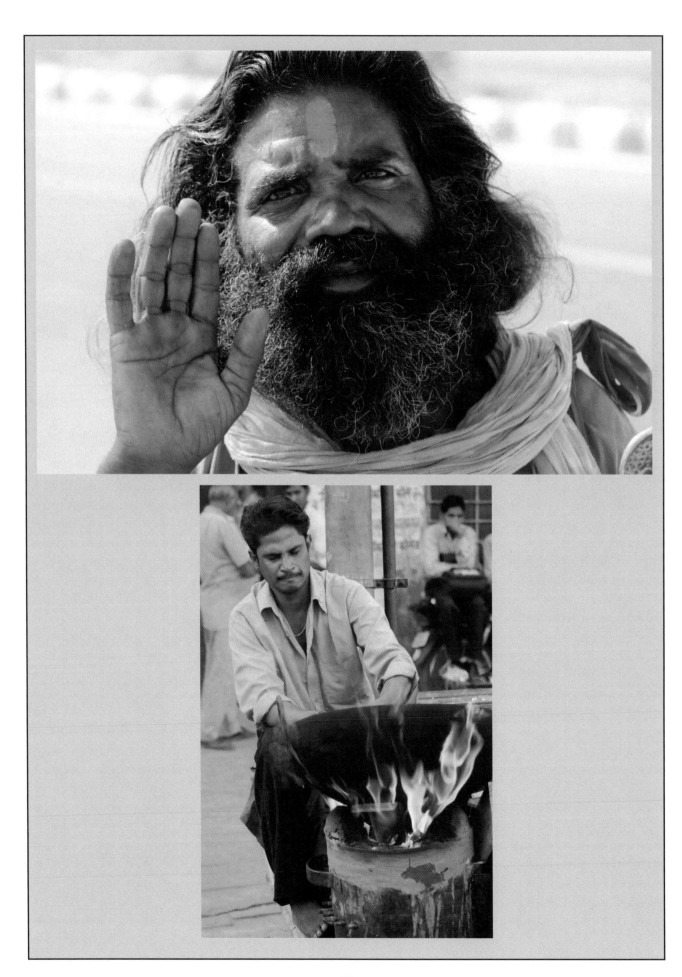

That Tullman Charm

10:00 p.m., Jaipur: As a photographer, Jaipur was my favorite city.

This city of three million people is a bright, colorful pink. The shops are loaded with rich silks, sparkling gems, and hand-carved marble, and the people are friendly and visually expressive.

The Moghal ruler, Sawai Jai Singh, designed the city in the early 1700s. He was a renowned mathematician and astronomer, and his precise mind is reflected in the orderly rectangular layout and wide dividing roads of the city.

Outside the Pink City

71

He also designed and built spectacular astronomical observatories called *Jantar Mantars*, which translates to "the formula of instruments."

The Jaipur Jantar Mantar, with its enormous stone structures, appears almost surreally out of the ground near the center of the city. While it looks like a twenty-first-century architectural project, it is actually a working astronomical instrument from the eighteen century, capable of exactly measuring planetary positions and reading time precisely to one second.

Jai Singh was given the title *Sawai*. which means "one and one quarter," because the emperor was impressed with all Jai Singh could do: 125 percent of the typical ruler. His palace flies a full-sized flag below a quarter-sized flag to commemorate his capacity.

Dubbing him "Sawai Glen," our guide, Veena, declared she had never had to work so hard to stay up with a client on a tour—that Glen was "one and a quarter."

Glen seemed quite pleased with this moniker and mentioned it to several women passing by.

Jai Singh also constructed an enormous summer palace not far from the Pink City, to which he and his several hundred wives would retreat to during the hot season.

Our Guide in Jaipur - Veena

Damn, They Sell Carpets in Jaipur Too*

*- See also "Kashmiri Rug Merchants," page 16.

11:00 p.m., Jaipur: Two weeks before we arrived, an elephant ride in Jaipur had ended in a fatality. All rides had been canceled—unless you are traveling with Exotic Journeys. Their guides can do the impossible.

So giddy up, elephant boys!!

Inside the elephant garage

11:30 p.m., Jaipur: I've found every day in India to be so filled with interesting discoveries that I've fallen six to seven posts behind on the blog. Having only dial-up access in Jaipur didn't help.

I'm not sure why India seems so intense an experience. It may be that with 1.1.billion people, there's just four times the activity of the U.S.

It may be because that giant population occupies an area one-third the size of America, so everything is more compressed.

Or it could just be just traveling with Glen Tullman, who can squeeze more adventure out of twenty-four hours than most people can find in a month. There is a special force about him that I've started calling "**GLENERGY**."

With Glen, sightseeing is more like a drive-by shooting. Nearing our destination, he asks the driver to slow down. Locking and loading our four cameras, we pull alongside our "target"; he orders a "stop" and we spring from both sides of the car.

Moving quickly in a slightly crouched position, we approach the subject at different angles— known as the "diagonal cross-shooting pattern"— ensuring that while we are taking *exactly* the same picture, one will have the slightly better photo in terms of light or background.

With all cameras blazing, we shoot men, women, children and cows, spraying them with high-speed shutter clicks and electronic flashes.

Then springing back into the car, Glen tells our guide, "Okay, good. What's next?"

Clearly no Indian tour guides have before heard phrases like:

- "Is there anything we can do on the way to where we are going to do that would be worth doing?"
- "Can we jog through this museum?"
- "Do you know where the cell towers are in Jaipur? Can we stay close to them and still see everything?"
- "How fast do elephants go? Can they run? Can you make them run? Can you show me how you do that?"

I love Glen's pace, though probably few others would. I've coined the term **competitive sightseeing and attack photography** to capture the essence of traveling with Glen.

BTW, it turns out that for 1000 rupees elephants will, in fact, run—an experience I do not intend to repeat.

Coconut milk – the secret to Glenergy?

11:45 p.m., Jaipur: **Business is a family affair in India**. Over 90 percent of the business people we met (with the exception of people in high technology) were the of the fourth, fifth—even twelfth generation of their family to run the family business.

This is changing somewhat, as the current generation is not only more highly educated, but the engineering degrees are allowing kids to pursue more lucrative careers in IT services, biotechnology, software, etc. It's hard to keep them in the retail jewelry business when they have an MS in computer science.

When we were in Jaipur we had the pleasure of meeting the seventh generation of a family of **master puppeteers**. They produced a delightful, unique, and very funny puppet show after dinner at the Raj Palace hotel.

These puppeteers handcraft the puppets, develop the story lines, write original scores, and travel around performing their shows. The night we were there it was three brothers of a very large family who were performing out of a small tent and stage setup. They could not have been nicer and answered our many questions with lots of humor. After the show, they slept right on the hotel grounds in the tent, ready to perform the next day.

Hey…the puppet is a guy riding a camel, okay? Come on…

11:00 p.m., Bharatpur: These collared owls are but one example of the more than 400 species of birds that are found in the Keoladeo Ghana National Park in Bharatpur.

We stayed at a fabulous new resort in Bharatpur called **The Bagh**, and one of the co-owners, Vishnu Singh, gave us a terrific tour of the bird sanctuary. His family has been hosting the world's most serious birders on visits to this sanctuary for about fifty years. Vishnu quickly noted that Glen and I are not serious birders and he rose to the occasion by taking us on a high-speed rickshaw tour and photo shoot of Keoladeo in the ninety minutes before sunset.

11:30 p.m., Bharatpur: Rural India is beautiful. The air is clean, the farms fertile, the people friendly.

While poverty was visible in every rural town we passed through, so was the Indian commitment to educating the next generation.

In every village there were dozens and dozens of school children; in uniform, under the watchful eye of their teachers.

The rural India of tomorrow will certainly be better than the rural India of today.

11:00 p.m., Bharatpur: There is an Indian tendency, it seems to me, to make holy anything that is odd or unusual.

In India, wild monkeys are considered holy and having a bunch of monkeys climbing around your house is considered auspicious.

These monkeys are pretty aggressive. They bite and many have rabies. I mean no disrespect, but having them crawling all over the place strikes me as just odd and less than auspicious.

I'm fine with the cow thing and the wild boars in the road eating garbage and the elephants as SUVs and the holy pigeons, but I must draw the line at the monkeys…

Okay, well they are very cute.

9:30 p.m., Agra: The electricity goes out several times a day in India, but the people are used to it and all businesses and most middle-class homes have UPS backup and individual power generators. While the Indians see reliable energy as a function of the government, they don't sit around waiting for it to get fixed or blaming someone. No one saw this as somehow George Bush's fault (except Glen).

The momentary loss of power hit Glen one afternoon. He was like this for about ten minutes and then made a complete recovery.

A Momentary Loss of Glenergy

10:00 p.m., Agra: Hello, my name is Bob and I'm a Taj Mahalic.

HI...BOB!!!

11:00 p.m., Agra: **When you first arrive in India, you see cows everywhere**: in the street, in yards, walking through vendor areas along the road. To Hindus, the cow is a sacred animal, and although disconcerting at first, after a while I sort of liked seeing these friendly, peaceful cows.

Something you don't notice about this scene until you've been there awhile is there is no cow manure. **One would expect to see excrement all over the place, but au contraire.**

The reason is **cow dung is an excellent energy source**. According to Glen, cows are very inefficient processors of food, so the dung is rich in organic material. (He learned this at Oxford.)

Mix the dung with a little straw, a pinch of dirt, air dry, and voila: the cow pie becomes the fuel patty. There is an entire industry built around the collection, processing, drying, distribution, and sale of dung.

So the fuel patty industry workers have jobs, the streets are kept very clean and free from odor, and the customer gets an excellent source of cheap, alternative energy for heat and cooking.

If one thinks of cow dung as merely organic material that has passed largely unprocessed through the cow, perhaps it's not so hard to imagine rolling, patting, and selling fuel patties. Then again…

Leave it to Indian resourcefulness to turn a mess into a profitable business.

As the saying goes, **"If life hands you a cow pie, make a fuel patty."**

Cow Patty Production

Bake in high heat until dry

Store in dry, well-ventilated area

95

I Had a Sudden Burst of GLENERGY

11:00 p.m., Agra: In India, every transaction—EVERY transaction—is negotiated. Merchandise, cab fare, restaurant bills, and wedding dowries; the list is endless.

As our guide, Vishnu explained, **"In India, we bargain to the level of the individual vegetable purchase."**

While awkward and uncomfortable to most Americans, that level of negotiating can be quite valuable.

Hotmail founder Sabeer Bhatia, a California transplant from Bangalore, credited the bargaining skills he learned in vegetable markets at home for getting Microsoft to push its acquisition price for his company from $160 million to $400 million. Bill Gates' eyeteeth were floating in tea with that deal.

Here are a few rules for bargaining on the buy-side when in India:

Rule #1 - The true price of any item is what you pay. There are no suggested retail prices in India. Nothing is labeled, so it pays to talk with several vendors before making a significant purchase.

Rule #2 - Try for 70% off. Don't accept less than 30 percent off.

Rule #3 - Make them show lots of merchandise. If it is a rug merchant, you want the demo guys sweating profusely before you make your first offer. Get the vendor to "invest" in the transaction—emotion, time, and energy.

Rule #4 - Offer on one item at a time. If you plan to buy a couple things, DON'T let on at the outset. Act like you intend to buy only one item, if that much. Get the seller to give you prices on each item; play one item off another to show you are looking for the lower price point.

Rule #5 - Wait for the pad of paper. Every Indian salesperson has a pad of paper and a pencil that they pull out when the bargaining gets a bit more serious. Though they write down the price for an item, this is only the starting point. (Remember Rule #2.)

Rule #6 - Say "TOO HIGH" a lot. Don't even start negotiating until the salesman has scratched through the initial price and lowered it at least twice. I found that simply staring in silence at the pad of paper for a long time would result in the vendor cutting the price.

Rule # 7 - Imply a bundled purchase. Okay, now that the price has been cut 25-30 percent, ask the salesman what deal he would give you if you buy two items. Expect 5 percent off. Ask for three items; get another 5 percent. Then add a very expensive fourth item— one which you do not intend to buy. This will excite the vendor and he will do a bunch of calculations that you will be unable to follow. The price will come down for the expensive item as well as for the other items you intend to buy. Lock those prices and drop the expensive item.

At this point you should have been able to shave close to 50 percent off the initial price. Most Americans generally are satisfied at this point and close the deal.

If you have time and patience, there are **6 more bargaining rules** that you can follow to get 70 percent off. For 5000 rupees, I'll email those rules to you.

Otherwise, you'll notice I have added a **Tip Jar** to my blog. No obligation—"as you like" as they say in India.

BUT you should know, I have just saved you a bundle on your first trip to India. So…as you like….

Before the transaction   After the deal is done

One final point: No matter what price you pay, if the sales guy is smiling when you leave, guess who won.

8:00 p.m., Memphis: On my last night in India I became violently ill at the Delhi Airport. This had both its good and bad aspects.

THE GOOD

1- The security clearance process, which normally takes nearly two hours, lasted less than five minutes—although I felt badly about barfing on the people in line ahead of me.

2- Medical care at midnight in the Delhi airport was absolutely superb. They even have a fully stocked pharmacy with state-controlled prices. No need to bargain!

3- The people in the first class lounge were so very quick to let me have the couch, both chairs on either side, and lots of room to breathe. They could not have been more thoughtful or kind

THE BAD

1- Twenty-six hours on an airplane with excruciating abdominal pain and a very bad taste in my mouth

2- A week to recover back in the U.S.

3- A few scowling people on the airplane pointing and whispering "that's him" or "he's the one."

Need I say more?

So what happened that caused this problem?

Well, when Glen was traveling with me, he enforced a **strict "no weird Indian food"** policy. But then, Glen left a day ahead of me and I could not control my desire for some **"authentic Indian street cuisine"**.

This was not smart. I don't know if it was the spicy "take the back of your head off" Indian dish, or if it was the delicious milkshake-like yogurt drink called a **"Sweet Lassi"**. How could I resist a few of those babies?

I do know that, contrary to its aggressive (some might say misleading) advertising, I cannot recommend to you the Shalimar Foods establishment when you are in Delhi. Perhaps the pharmacy next door was a clue…

10:00 p.m., Memphis: Today is my last post from our trip to India.

I hope the blog speaks for itself, so I'll add only a few wrap-up comments.

I have several people to thank for making this trip so extraordinary:

1- I'm very grateful to **my wife, Janice** , and **my daughters, Elizabeth and Meredith**, for letting me be away for so long and for so graciously accepting all of the presents I brought back from India, particularly the four Indian carpets.

2- I want to thank **my sister-in-law—Lynn Cutter**, SVP at National Geographic—for her travel advice. The National Geographic connections proved invaluable and I would highly recommend the National Geographic Journey through India itinerary.

3- Thanks to **Franceen and Tammy** at Allscripts for coordinating my travels with Glen's schedule and for inserting and extracting him from India like Delta Force commanders.

4- Our trip was made very special by **Raj Singh** and the staff of his business, Exotic Journeys. I would highly recommend his company for any travel you might consider in India. His firm is simply outstanding. Raj can be contacted at **exotic@del2.vsnl.net.in**.

5- Finally, I want to thank **Glen Tullman**, who made a great trip to India into a truly extraordinary, high-bandwidth, high-speed experience of a remarkable country and culture.

India was a profound journey for me—so profound, in fact, that I'm going back on January 20 for another week or so. Though I plan to continue sightseeing, this trip will be geared much more toward assessing both new business ventures and real estate investments in Bangalore.

My belief is India over the next five years will be a combination of San Francisco during the Gold Rush, Texas during the oil boom, Silicon Valley in the early 1980s, and America in the 1950s.

India is exotic, exciting, and inspiring, but most of all, **India today is about opportunity**, and I personally plan to capitalize on it.

Robert A. Compton has had a 25 year career creating, financing and managing new ventures. Entrepreneur, angel investor and professional venture capitalist, he has been active in a wide range of businesses including software, telecommunication services, healthcare services and medical devices. Compton has served on more than three dozen corporate and philanthropic boards, including Allscripts Healthcare Solutions, Interactive Intelligence, Sofamor Danek Group, the Ewing Marion Kauffman Foundation and the Plough Foundation. He holds an MBA from Harvard Business School, a BA from Principia College and an Honorary Doctorate from the Rose-Hulman Institute of Technology. [www.robertacompton.com]

Printed in the United States
65181LVS00001B